CARING

TARANTULA AS PET

A BEGINNERS GUIDE TO THEIR HABITAT, CARE, DIET, HEALTH, MANAGEMENT, REQUIREMENTS, OWNERSHIP AND MORE

REYNARD MARTIN

Copyright© 2025 **REYNARD MARTIN**

All rights reserved. No part of this work may be reproduced, distributed, or transmitted in any form or by any means, including photocopying, recording, or other electronic or mechanical methods without the prior written permission of the author

Table of Contents

INTRODUCTION 5

CHAPTER 1 15

SELECTING THE RIGHT TARANTULA SPECIES 15

CHAPTER 2 26

SETTING UP THE PERFECT HABITAT 26

CHAPTER 3 37

FEED YOUR TARANTULA 37

CHAPTER 4 48

HANDLING AND INTERACTING WITH YOUR TARANTULA 48

CHAPTER 5 59

HEALTH AND WELLNESS OF YOUR TARANTULA 59

CHAPTER 6 72

BREEDING AND REPRODUCTION OF TARANTULAS 72

CHAPTER 7 82

SAFETY AND PRECAUTIONS: HANDLING VENOMOUS TARANTULAS 82

CHAPTER 8 92

Common Misconceptions and Myths about Tarantulas 92

CONCLUSION 101

The Benefits of Tarantula Ownership 101

Introduction

Tarantulas are among the most fascinating and misunderstood species in the world. These big, hairy spiders frequently inspire strong reactions, ranging from horror to interest. While many people connect spiders with negativity or danger, tarantulas are actually rather peaceful and non-aggressive when properly cared for. Their fascinating activity, distinct appearance, and low maintenance requirements make them a wonderful choice for a pet, particularly for those looking for a more unconventional companion.

In this book, we'll look at why tarantulas make excellent pets, as well as their natural history, which will help us understand their behavior and demands. Understanding their native habitat and evolution is critical to guaranteeing their success in captivity.

Why Get a Tarantula as a Pet?
When it comes to pets, many people think of typical animals such as dogs, cats, and even fish. However, tarantulas provide a whole other experience—one that is both satisfying and enlightening. There are several reasons why individuals pick tarantulas as pets,

whether they are experienced spider lovers or first-time pet owners.

- Low maintenance

One of the most enticing parts of owning a tarantula is its low care requirements. Tarantulas are autonomous creatures, unlike dogs and cats, which demand continual attention. They do not require daily walks, constant attention, or a lot of maintenance. As long as their habitat is correctly set up and they have food and water, they are relatively self-sufficient.

Tarantulas do not require frequent feedings; they can be fed once a week or less frequently, depending on the species and age of the tarantula. This makes them perfect for those who do not have the time or resources to care for a high-maintenance pet. If you have a busy lifestyle, a tarantula could be the ideal pet.

- Fascinating to observe

Tarantulas are fascinating to watch. Unlike ordinary pets, they move slowly and deliberately, capturing the observer's attention. Their hunting strategies, web-spinning abilities, and interactions with their surroundings offer limitless opportunities for learning and discovery. Whether it's watching them hunt for prey or studying their unique molting process, there's always something going on in the tarantula enclosure.

- Educational value

Tarantulas provide educational benefits, particularly to youngsters and young people. These critters provide a glimpse into the world of arachnology—the study of spiders—and might be a good introduction to the field of entomology. Observing the tarantula's life cycle, behavior, and care requirements can teach valuable lessons in responsibility, patience, and respect for all living creatures.

Tarantulas are also fascinating in a scientific sense. They have a long evolutionary history, and their morphological and behavioural adaptations make them excellent survivors. Understanding the evolution of tarantulas can provide insight into the greater world of natural history.

- A Unique and Low-Stressed Pet

Tarantulas are an excellent alternative for anyone seeking a more calm, low-stress pet. They are naturally solitary animals, and they do not require regular interaction with humans. Their placid temperament and moderate level of activity make them less prone to generate anxiety or stress in a home. Tarantulas, unlike dogs and cats, do not demand attention, make noise, or take up a lot of room.

Tarantulas, unlike many mammals, are not territorial or hostile. As long as they are not provoked, they are pleased to stay in their enclosures, making them an ideal alternative for anyone who do not want an extremely social pet.

- Low-cost care

Tarantulas are not only low-maintenance, but also relatively affordable to care for. The initial setup costs for their habitat vary according on the species and size, but once the enclosure is completed, the continuing costs are low. You won't have to spend a lot of money on food or medical care, and your tarantula can have a long and healthy life if properly cared for.

Furthermore, many tarantula species are widely available for purchase, indicating that they are not endangered and are frequently raised in captivity. This lowers the need to capture them in the wild and allows pet owners to enjoy them in a sustainable manner.

- A Conversation Starter

Having a tarantula as a pet can also spark interesting conversations. They are peculiar creatures that frequently surprise those who are unfamiliar with them. Owning a tarantula challenges conventional assumptions and allows you to educate others about these amazing spiders. Many individuals, whether friends, family, or guests, are fascinated about tarantulas, providing an opportunity for pet owners to share their knowledge and experiences.

- suitable for small spaces

Another major advantage of owning a tarantula is that they do not require much space. Tarantulas flourish in compact confines, unlike larger pets like dogs and birds. A well-sized tank or terrarium will suffice to suit their requirements, making them excellent for those who live in apartments, dorms, or other small living spaces. Because of their modest size and limited activity, they don't need a yard or a vast living space to be content.

- A diverse range of species

Tarantulas appear in a range of species, each with its own unique traits. Some tarantulas are noted for their vibrant hues, such as the green bottle blue tarantula, while others are more understated but no less fascinating. Whether you choose a small species or a giant, spectacular one, there is a tarantula to suit your preferences and personality.

While having a spider may seem scary to some, tarantulas may make excellent pets for those who are ready to put in the time and effort to care for them. Tarantulas provide a one-of-a-kind pet experience due to their low maintenance needs, educational value, and distinctive appeal.

A Short History of Tarantulas in the Wild
Tarantulas are members of the order Araneae, which includes all spiders, including the family Theraphosidae. These ancient organisms have a lengthy and illustrious history stretching back hundreds of millions of years. To better understand the behavior and demands of tarantulas as pets, consider their natural habitat and the evolution that has turned them into the interesting creatures they are today.

Early Evolution and Fossil Record
Tarantulas are among the world's oldest spiders. Tarantulas have been around for almost 300 million years, according to fossil data, with some of the earliest fossils discovered in modern-day

Europe. This places them in the late Paleozoic epoch, when huge insects ruled the planet. During this time, oxygen levels in the atmosphere were significantly higher, allowing for the development of bigger arthropods such as spiders.

As evolution evolved, the ancestors of modern tarantulas adapted to a wide range of environments. These spiders evolved into big, burrowing monsters equipped with unique traits for hunting and survival in a variety of habitats. Tarantulas' unusual size and hair-covered bodies are regarded to be evolutionary adaptations that allowed them to better protect themselves from predators and catch prey.

Global Distribution

Tarantulas live on every continent except Antarctica. They thrive in warm, tropical, and subtropical climates, with a considerable presence in Central and South America, Africa, Asia, and the Mediterranean. Their habitats range from lush rainforests and deserts to scrublands and grasslands, all of which provide them with warmth, food, and shelter.

Various species have adapted to their habitats, resulting in a vast range of sizes, colors, and behaviors. Some tarantulas, like as the

Mexican redknee tarantula, live in trees, whilst others, like the Chilean rose tarantula, live on the ground. Despite their diversity, most tarantulas have some characteristics, including as their big size, slow motions, and unusual leg span.

Physical and Behavioral Adaptations

Tarantulas have developed a number of extraordinary morphological and behavioral adaptations that allow them to live in the wild. Tarantulas are well-known for their potent venom. While the venom of most tarantulas is not lethal to humans, it is strong enough to immobilize victims. Their venom contains enzymes that help break down the prey's tissues, allowing the tarantula to digest it more easily. This adaptation enables tarantulas to catch and consume prey that is frequently larger than themselves, such as insects, tiny amphibians, and even small reptiles.

Tarantulas are also known for their urticating hairs, which are small, barbed hairs that may be released from their belly when threatened. These hairs are not venomous, but they can irritate and bother potential predators. This protective system is especially effective at deterring larger predators that may try to prey on the tarantula.

Tarantulas are also recognized for their ability to grow through the molting process. Tarantulas, unlike mammals, must lose their exoskeleton (via a process called as ecdysis) to accommodate their developing bodies. This procedure is a necessary element of their life cycle and an adaptation that helps them to live and thrive in a range of settings.

Hunting and Feeding Behavior

Tarantulas are opportunistic hunters who excel at ambushing their prey. To catch their prey, they use a combination of stealth and speed, usually hiding in a tunnel or crevice until prey approaches. Once the prey is within range, the tarantula will lunge and inject its venom into it, paralyzing it and allowing the spider to consume it gradually.

Tarantulas are not aggressive predators; instead, they preserve energy by waiting for prey to approach them. This hunting method is well adapted to their surroundings, where prey can be scarce and difficult to locate. Their ability to go for extended periods of time without food makes them extremely flexible, allowing them to live in environments where food is not always plentiful.

Reproduction and Life Cycles

Tarantula reproduction is perhaps another fascinating aspect of their natural history. These spiders have elaborate courtship rituals in which the male makes a variety of movements and drumming patterns to lure a mate. If she accepts him, he will mate with her. Following mating, the female lays a clutch of eggs, which she guards until the spiderlings hatch. Tarantulas have a long life cycle, with females lasting up to 20 years in the wild and males normally living for roughly 5 years.

Understanding the natural history and evolution of tarantulas provides useful information on their behavior and needs as pets. Their lengthy history of survival and adaptation to varied environments has turned them into intriguing creatures capable of thriving in a wide range of habitats, including those we make for them in captivity. Whether you're a seasoned enthusiast or a first-time owner, learning more about the tarantula's natural habitat can help you give the finest care for these magnificent spiders.

Chapter 1

Selecting the Right Tarantula Species

Tarantulas are a varied group of spiders, with more than 1,000 species found around the world. Each species has distinct qualities that make it more or less suitable for various types of pet owners. Selecting the appropriate tarantula species is critical for anyone considering keeping one as a pet. Size, temperament, and care requirements all play an important role in selecting which species is most suited to your lifestyle and level of experience.

In this chapter, we'll go over the important elements to consider while selecting the proper tarantula species, with a focus on the best species for novices. We'll also look at temperament and size differences, which can have a significant impact on your tarantula ownership experience.

Best species for beginners

For individuals who are new to maintaining tarantulas, choosing a species that is easy to care for and non-aggressive is critical. Some tarantula species are more tolerant of beginning blunders, but others demand a more expert hand. If you're just starting off, selecting the proper species will guarantee a happy and satisfying experience. Here are some of the most suitable species for beginners:

1. Chilean Rose Tarantula (Grammostola Rosea)

The Chilean rose tarantula is one of the most popular species among novices. This species, known for its docile temperament, is frequently suggested to individuals new to the world of tarantulas. It is an excellent choice due to its manageable size, placid disposition, and minimal care requirements.

Key features:

- Tarantulas are normally medium-sized, with leg spans of 4-5 inches.
- Temperament: Generally calm and gentle, but individual personalities can vary. It is less likely to engage in hostile behavior than other species.
- Care Instructions: Chilean rose tarantulas are hardy and adaptive. They flourish in a range of conditions and are tolerant of temperature and humidity fluctuations. They

enjoy a dry, somewhat humid atmosphere and may thrive with low humidity.
- Lifespan: Females can live for 10-15 years, but males usually live for 3-5 years.

The Chilean rose tarantula's placid attitude and tolerance to various care settings make it a good choice for new tarantula owners. Though it is not as active or flamboyant as other species, its gentle nature and simple maintenance requirements make it an excellent choice for novices.

2. Mexican Redknee Tarantulas (Brachypelma smithi)

The Mexican redknee tarantula is a wonderful choice for novices. This species, known for its spectacular look and rather tranquil behavior, is quite popular among tarantula fans. It is a fantastic species for anyone who want a gorgeous, low-maintenance pet that is easy to care for.

Key features:

- Size: A medium-sized tarantula with a leg span of 5-6 inches.

- Temperament: Generally quiet and slow-moving. It is one of the most docile tarantula species and is known to tolerate handling more than other species.
- Care Requirements: Mexican redknees thrive in warm, dry climates with some humidity. They prefer a slightly moist substrate, but do not require extreme humidity. Regular feeding and misting will keep them in good health.
- Females can live for up to 20 years, whilst males have a lower lifespan of approximately 5-7 years.

The Mexican redknee tarantula's tolerance for handling, as well as its stunning black and orange appearance, making it popular among newcomers. Furthermore, it is relatively hardy and adaptable to different settings, making it easier to care for than other species. This species is also more active than other of the more sedentary species, making it an entertaining pet to watch.

3. Pink Toe Tarantulas (Avicularia avicularia)

The pink toe tarantula is another popular species among beginners, especially those looking for an arboreal (tree-dwelling) species. This species is recognized for its stunning, brilliant hues and graceful movement. While not as prevalent as the Chilean rose or the Mexican redknee, the pink toe is an excellent alternative for new tarantula owners looking for something unique.

Key features:

- Size: Medium, with a leg span of 4-5 inches.
- Temperament: Generally peaceful, but may be more skittish than other species. They are highly energetic and frequently move quickly and erratically. Despite their flightier behavior, they are not violent and rarely bite.
- Pink toe tarantulas require a humid climate as well as a climbable habitat. Providing vertical space, such as branches or cork bark, is critical for their health. They also demand a high humidity level of 70-80% and temperatures ranging from 75-85°F (24-29°C).
- Lifespan: Females can live for up to 8-10 years, while males normally live only 2-3 years.

Pink toe tarantulas are an excellent choice for novices seeking a more active and visually appealing species. While they demand slightly different care circumstances than terrestrial species, they are still rather simple to keep, especially if you can match their humidity and space needs. Their tree-dwelling habits make them unusual and interesting to watch as they ascend and wander within their cages.

4. Curly Hair Tarantula (Tliltocatl Albopilosus)

The curly hair tarantula is another excellent choice for novices, because to its placid demeanor and distinct appearance. Its curling, hairy legs distinguish it as one of the most unusual tarantula species, which has contributed to its appeal among pet owners.

Key features:

- Size: Medium, with a leg span of 4-5 inches.
- Temperament: Generally relaxed and easygoing. It is one of the most docile tarantulas and easy to handle. While some may be wary, most curly hair tarantulas tolerate moderate handling.
- Care Requirements: Curly hair tarantulas enjoy a dry habitat with occasional humidity. It requires a burrowing substrate and should be kept in a temperature range of 75-85°F (24-29°C). Humidity levels should be moderate, between 60 and 70%.

- Lifespan: Females can live up to 12-15 years, while males normally survive only 3-5 years.

Curly hair tarantulas are well-known for their ease of care and tolerance to handling. Their peaceful demeanor and distinctive appearance make them an intriguing option for first-time tarantula owners. Curly hair tarantulas, like many other starting species, are hardy and versatile, allowing them to survive in a variety of environments with little work from the owner.

5. Brazilian black tarantula (Grammostola pulchra).

The Brazilian black tarantula is another beginner-friendly species that is frequently suggested for its placid behavior and gorgeous beauty. It is distinguished by its stunning, shiny black body and generally non-aggressive disposition.

Key features:

- Size is medium to large, with a leg span of 6-7 inches.
- Temperament: Very gentle and calm. This species is noted for its patience and tolerance of handling, making it an ideal choice for owners looking for a tarantula that is both visually appealing and calm.

- Brazilian black tarantulas require relatively dry conditions with moderate humidity. They should be housed in a large enclosure with sufficient substrate for burrowing. They flourish in temperatures ranging from 75°F to 85°F (24-29°C).
- Lifespan: Females can live up to 15-20 years, but males only live 5-7 years.

The Brazilian black tarantula's gentle attitude and attractive looks make it an excellent choice for new tarantula owners searching for a larger species. This species is hardy and versatile, making it simpler to care for than more temperamental species. Its extended lifetime makes it an ideal long-term companion for people who are dedicated to caring for a pet tarantula.

Differences in temperment and size

When selecting a tarantula species, it is critical to consider not only the care requirements but also the temperament and size of the animal. These elements can significantly impact your experience as a pet owner.

- Temperament

Tarantulas' disposition varies tremendously. Some species are placid and easy to handle, while others are more shy and aggressive. Understanding different species' temperaments will help you decide which one is ideal for your lifestyle.

Docile Species: The Chilean rose, Mexican redknee, and Brazilian black are recognized for their peaceful and docile behavior. These tarantulas are more tolerant of handling and less aggressive overall. They are ideal pets for novices who want a calm companion who is not prone to biting or defensive behavior.

Some tarantula species, such as the pink toe and the Gooty sapphire, are known to be skittish or flighty. These tarantulas are more inclined to flee when disturbed and may engage in defensive behavior such as flicking urticating hairs. While they are not normally aggressive, their sensitivity to handling makes them unsuitable for beginners.

protective Species: several tarantulas, particularly larger species such as the Goliath birdeater and several Heteroscodra species, can be more protective. They may move quickly and bite if they feel threatened. These species are often not suitable for inexperienced owners.

- Size

Tarantula size is another critical thing to consider. Larger tarantulas might be scary for new owners, although smaller species may be easier to care. Here's a summary of how size can influence your decision:

tiny to Medium-Sized Species: Most beginner-friendly tarantulas, including as the Chilean rose, Mexican redknee, and curly hair, are tiny to medium in size. These species often have leg spans of 4-6 inches, which makes them easier to handle and care for. Their enclosures demand less room and are easier to feed and maintain.

Larger species, such the Goliath birdeater or the Brazilian salmon pink, can have legs that are 8 inches or longer. While these species are stunning, they require larger enclosures and are more difficult to manage because to their size and power. Their eating requirements are likewise higher, since they require larger prey items.

Tiny Species: Smaller tarantulas, such as Grammostola pulchra or dwarf species from the genus Brachypelma, are perfect for individuals seeking a smaller pet. These species may appear less threatening, but they still require proper care to thrive.

Choosing the proper tarantula species is a critical step in your pet-ownership adventure. You can choose a species that matches your level of experience and preferences by taking into account traits like temperament, size, and care requirements. For beginners, species such as the Chilean rose, Mexican redknee, and curly hair tarantula are frequently the best options since they are docile, easy to care for, and visually appealing. Understanding the differences in temperament and size will allow you to make an informed decision and have a rewarding and long-term relationship with your new tarantula pet.

Chapter 2

Setting up the perfect habitat

Creating the proper environment for a tarantula is critical to its health and survival. These critters may be low-maintenance, but they still need certain conditions to survive. Providing a home that closely resembles their original environment helps keep your tarantula healthy, comfortable, and stress-free. Whether you're housing a beginner-friendly species like a Chilean rose or a more specialist species like a pink toe tarantula, the requirements for its home are nearly same. In this section, we'll look at the most important aspects of creating the ideal habitat, such as terrarium necessities, creating a safe and natural environment, and maintaining proper humidity, lighting, and ventilation.

Terrarium Essentials: Size, Substrate, and Temperature
Before bringing your new tarantula home, make sure you have everything ready. A suitable terrarium setup is necessary to ensure your tarantula's health and happiness. In this section, we'll cover the fundamentals of terrarium size, substrate, and

temperature regulation, three of the most crucial aspects of providing a pleasant environment for your tarantula.

Terrarium Size

The size of the terrarium you choose will be determined by your tarantula's species and age. While tarantulas do not require much space, their cages should be large enough for them to walk around, burrow, or climb, depending on whether they are arboreal (tree-dwelling) or terrestrial. To keep your tarantula from feeling cramped or anxious, choose a proper enclosure size.

- Small Tarantulas: If you are harboring a juvenile or smaller species, a smaller enclosure is sufficient. A 5 to 10-gallon tank or similar-sized container will do. Juvenile tarantulas require less area than adults, so a smaller habitat makes it easier for them to find food and shelter.
- Adult Tarantulas: For larger species or adult tarantulas, you need to give a larger enclosure. A 10 to 20-gallon tank or terrarium is frequently ideal, providing enough room for the tarantula to move. A 10-gallon tank is usually adequate for most adult species, but larger species, like the Goliath birdeater or Brazilian salmon pink, may require an enclosure of 20 gallons or more.

When choosing a terrarium, consider the species' natural habits. Arboreal species, such as the pink toe tarantula, require vertical room to climb. These species require a taller container, whereas terrestrial animals prefer a tank that is longer and more horizontally spacious.

Substrate

Substrate is the material that lines the bottom of your tarantula's container, allowing it to burrow, make webs, and relax. Choosing the appropriate substrate is critical since it impacts your tarantula's comfort, as well as the humidity and cleanliness of the habitat.

Coco Coir: One of the most popular substrates for tarantulas is coco coir, which is made from the fibrous husk of coconuts. Coco coir retains moisture efficiently, making it ideal for species that require high humidity. It's also safe, natural, and simple to maintain. Coco coir is a good alternative for terrestrial animals due to its ability to promote digging.

Sphagnum moss is another alternative for good moisture retention. It works especially well for species that require high humidity, such as arboreal tarantulas. Moss may help create a more natural appearance and give a comfy surface for your tarantula to lay on.

Peat Moss and Topsoil: For species that prefer drier environments, peat moss or topsoil can be beneficial. These substrates can absorb moisture and aid to maintain a dry atmosphere, which is good to species such as the Chilean rose tarantula.

Sand and Gravel: While sand and gravel appear to be suitable options for desert species, they are generally not advised for tarantulas since they lack moisture retention and digging skills. A thin layer of sand, blended with various substrates, can be used as a decorative layer.

Terrestrial species require a substrate depth of about 2-4 inches to enable for burrowing. Arboreal species do not require a deep substrate layer, although they do benefit from a shallow layer for web-building.

Temperature
Tarantulas are cold-blooded, which means they rely on external heat sources to keep their body temperature stable. Maintaining

an appropriate temperature in their enclosure is critical for their digestion, metabolism, and overall health. Tarantulas have slightly variable temperature requirements, however there are broad rules that apply to the majority of species.

Optimal Temperature Range: Most tarantula species survive in temperatures between 75°F and 85°F (24°C to 29°C). Keeping the enclosure within this range ensures that your tarantula remains active and healthy. Too low temperatures might produce lethargy and decreased eating behavior, but excessively high temperatures can cause stress or even heatstroke.

Heating Elements: If your home is too cold or your tarantula needs a certain temperature range, you may need to use a heating element. Common options include under-tank heaters, heat mats, and ceramic heat emitters. Use a thermometer to check the temperature on a regular basis, and never position the heat source directly on the tank's bottom to avoid overheating. Always look for a steady heat source that will keep the temperature stable.

Temperature Gradients: Some tarantula species benefit from temperature gradients, which occur when one side of the enclosure is warmer than another. This allows your tarantula to move to the optimum location for its needs at any given time. To generate this gradient effect, place a heat source on one side of the tank while leaving the other at ambient temperature.

Developing a Safe and Natural Environment
In addition to the fundamental requirements of size, substrate, and temperature, it is critical to establish a habitat that is as natural and safe as possible for your tarantula. Mimicking the creature's natural environment not only improves its comfort and well-being, but also its overall health.

Hiding Places and Shelter:
Tarantulas are inherently reclusive creatures. They prefer a secure hiding area where they may withdraw and feel comfortable. Providing a hiding space in the habitat reduces stress and makes your tarantula feel secure.

Burrowing Species: To construct hiding places for terrestrial species such as the Chilean rose or curly hair tarantula, use bits of cork bark, coconut shells, or half-buried flower pots. These products provide a private space for your tarantula to retreat to.

Furthermore, supplying adequate substrate for burrowing enables the spider to construct its own hideout.

Arboreal species, such as the pink toe tarantula, can use branches, vines, or tree bark to build climbing structures and hiding places. These species prefer to stay off the ground, therefore a vertical layout with variety of hiding areas at various heights will be beneficial.

To provide your tarantula with options, provide hiding locations throughout the habitat. This reduces the likelihood of stress, particularly during molting or feeding.

Decor & Enrichment:
Adding natural décor, such as plants, rocks, and branches, can both beautify and enrich your tarantula's home. These features help to imitate a natural habitat, providing more options for climbing, hiding, and webbing.

Live Plants: Some tarantula keepers choose to use live plants in their enclosures. Live plants serve to regulate humidity and improve the beauty of the habitat. However, live plants require proper care, and some tarantula species can upset or damage them. Consider hardy plants such as pothos, ferns, and mosses that can flourish under high humidity and low light conditions.

Non-Living Décor: Artificial plants and plastic branches are ideal for people looking for low-maintenance décor. These features offer similar benefits to living plants without the need for further maintenance. Just be sure to utilize non-toxic materials and avoid sharp edges that could damage your tarantula.

Humidity, Lighting and Ventilation

Maintaining appropriate humidity, lighting, and ventilation is critical for providing a comfortable and healthy environment for your tarantula. These aspects contribute to the general climate of the enclosure and help to simulate the natural environment of the species you are keeping.

Humidity:

Humidity is one of the most crucial components of a tarantula's habitat, particularly for species from tropical or subtropical regions. Humidity levels should be constantly controlled to keep your tarantula healthy.

Humidity Requirements: Each tarantula species has unique humidity requirements. For example, the pink toe tarantula, which is native to rainforests, needs greater humidity levels (about 70-80%), whereas the Chilean rose tarantula prefers a drier environment with humidity levels closer to 50-60%. Be sure to research your species' exact humidity requirements.

Maintaining Humidity: To maintain the correct humidity, spritz the enclosure with water on a regular basis. Be careful not to overdo it, since too much moisture can promote mold growth. To maintain humidity levels steady, consider using a hygrometer (a humidity measuring instrument). You can also use substrates like coco coir and sphagnum moss to help keep moisture in the cage.

Water Dish: Always have a shallow water dish for your tarantula to drink from. Tarantulas can drown if they fall into water, so make sure it is easily accessible but not too deep. Change the water on a regular basis to maintain it clean and debris-free.

Lighting:
Tarantulas are nocturnal species and do not require a particular lighting arrangement. Indeed, because these spiders prefer low-

light environments, bright lighting can create stress and confusion.

Natural Light: Place your tarantula's enclosure in a location that allows it to experience the natural day-night cycle. You do not need to offer additional lighting unless the enclosure is positioned in an extremely dark environment.

Avoiding Artificial Lighting: Bright lights can cause stress and disrupt your tarantula's natural behavior. If you need to illuminate the enclosure for viewing purposes, utilize low-intensity or indirect lighting.

Ventilation:
Proper ventilation is required to prevent the accumulation of mildew, bacteria, and hazardous gasses in the tarantula's habitat. Without proper airflow, the enclosure may become stifling and harmful for the tarantula.

Ventilation Holes: Make sure the enclosure has proper ventilation holes. These should be placed on the sides or top of the terrarium to allow air to move freely while maintaining the desired humidity levels. Make sure the holes are not too huge, as this may allow your tarantula to escape.

Airflow Management: Use a modest fan or vent to increase airflow in the room where the enclosure is housed. Avoid placing the enclosure in a drafty place or near an air conditioning vent, since unexpected temperature changes might stress the tarantula.

Creating the ideal habitat for your tarantula requires meticulous preparation and attention to detail. You can provide a secure, pleasant, and natural environment for your new pet by taking into account terrarium size, substrate selection, temperature, and humidity levels. Remember that tarantulas are incredibly adaptable organisms, yet they thrive best in habitats that closely resemble their natural environment. Whether you're harboring a terrestrial species like the Chilean rose or an arboreal species like the pink toe, the proper arrangement can keep your tarantula healthy, stress-free, and content for years.

Chapter 3

Feed Your Tarantula

Proper feeding is a critical element of tarantula care. Tarantulas are carnivorous creatures that feed on insects, tiny reptiles, and other invertebrates. A tarantula's diet must mimic this natural habit in order for them to stay healthy and grow as pets. This part will go over the several aspects of feeding your tarantula, such as what to feed it, how often to feed it, and how to provide enough hydration.

Feeding Your Tarantula: Insects and More
Tarantulas are opportunistic predators that eat insects, small rodents, amphibians, and, on occasion, small birds. When it comes to feeding your tarantula at home, there are a variety of prey items that will keep it healthy.

- Insects are the main diet

Most pet tarantulas will eat insects as their major food source since they are readily available, nutritious, and mirror the tarantula's natural hunting behavior. You can feed your tarantula a variety of insects, each with a unique nutritional profile.

Crickets are among the most common prey items for tarantulas. They are frequently available at pet stores and can be purchased both live and frozen. Crickets are a great source of protein, and most tarantulas enjoy hunting them. Crickets are heavy in fat, so don't overfeed them to your tarantula. If you use live crickets, make sure they are the right size—a larger cricket may overpower a smaller species.

Dubia roaches are another excellent food source for tarantulas. These roaches are abundant in protein and fat, making them suitable for most species. Dubia roaches are very easy to keep because they do not jump or climb, reducing the possibility of escapes in your home. They also have a long lifespan and reproduce easily, making them an ideal food source.

Mealworms are another common bug feeder for tarantulas. These worms are high in fat, so feed them sparingly. Mealworms are easy to keep and are an excellent choice for tarantulas in need of a supplemental food source. However, due to their high fat content, they should not comprise the majority of your tarantula's food.

Superworms: Superworms are larger than mealworms and make a good food source for larger tarantulas or species that require more regular feedings. They, like mealworms, should be eaten in moderation due to their high fat content. Tarantulas may struggle to collect smaller insects, thus superworms are an easier food source.

Grasshoppers and locusts are commonly used to feed larger tarantulas since they are more substantial than crickets or mealworms. Grasshoppers and locusts are nutritious, although they may be tough to find depending on where you live. They are particularly heavy in protein, making them ideal for species that demand larger meals.

Tarantulas may take fruit flies or house flies, particularly younger or smaller species. Fruit flies are ideal for feeding smaller species or spiderlings because they are small and easy for the tarantula to grasp. House flies can also be employed, albeit they are less nutritious than other insects.

Beetles and Other Invertebrates: To diversify your tarantula's diet, occasionally feed beetles such as the darkling beetle or other invertebrates such as caterpillars. These insects are often used to feed larger tarantulas, and they provide various forms of nutrition that can supplement the standard diet of crickets or roaches.

Tarantulas prefer live insects to pre-killed insects because they activate their natural hunting and predatory impulses. However, pre-killed insects can be fed, particularly if live prey is unavailable. Pre-killed insects should be freshly killed and free of preservatives, as decomposing food might harm your tarantula's health.

Other Food Options

While insects make up the majority of a tarantula's diet, they can also eat other foods on occasion.

Pinkie Mice: In the wild, giant tarantulas, like the Goliath birdeater and the Brazilian salmon pink, may hunt little rodents. Pinkie mice (newborn mice) are a great source of protein for larger tarantulas. These can be purchased frozen at pet stores and defrosted prior to feeding. Pinkie mice should not be eaten frequently because they are high in fat and can contribute to obesity if consumed regularly.

Other Small Vertebrates: Depending on the size of your tarantula, you can periodically give it small vertebrates such as geckos, frogs, and even hatchling reptiles. However, this should be uncommon because vertebrates may transmit diseases or parasites that can hurt your tarantula.

Eggs and Other Protein-Rich meals: Some tarantula owners like to give their animals tiny amounts of eggs or other protein-rich meals like cooked chicken. This is generally not suggested unless you have prior expertise, as eggs and cooked meat might result in imbalanced diets, and cooked meat may offer health hazards.

Feeding Frequency and Technique

Understanding how often and how to feed your tarantula might help you keep it healthy. Tarantulas, unlike more traditional pets, do not require regular meals and can go weeks or even months without feeding, particularly during molting.

- Feeding frequency

Feeding frequency varies depending on various things, including your tarantula's size and age, species, and if it is growing or molting. Here are some broad guidelines to follow:

Juvenile Tarantulas: Juveniles grow quickly and require more regular feedings to maintain their growth. Feeding juvenile tarantulas once every 2-3 days is generally advised. Because the tarantula is still developing its hunting and feeding abilities, you may need to provide smaller prey such as crickets or fruit flies.

Adult tarantulas have slower metabolisms and require less food. Adult tarantulas are normally fed once a week or every two weeks, depending on the species. Larger species may require larger prey and more frequent meals, although they do not consume as much as youngsters.

Tarantulas do not eat while they are molting. Tarantulas are extremely vulnerable while shedding their exoskeleton, therefore you should withhold food before and after the molt. Some species may go for several weeks without eating during this phase. To avoid tension, it's important not to serve meals during this time.

Overfeeding: While it is important to keep your tarantula well-nourished, excessive feeding can lead to obesity and other health issues. Feeding too frequently, particularly with high-fat meals such as mealworms, might lead your tarantula to grow overweight, resulting in molting issues or perhaps a shorter lifespan.

- Feeding Techniques

There are two main methods for feeding a pet tarantula: direct feeding and free-range feeding. Both strategies are effective, but they require specific precautions.

Direct feeding is the most usual way to feed tarantulas. This entails placing the prey in the enclosure right in front of the tarantula. It is critical to oversee feeding, particularly when introducing larger prey. To trigger the tarantula's hunting instincts, the prey should be alive and active. You can offer the prey to the tarantula with tongs or tweezers, or carefully position the insect within its grasp.

Advantages: This method allows you to see the tarantula's eating patterns and remove uneaten prey before it decomposes, which can cause mold or bacteria in the enclosure. It also lowers the likelihood of prey escaping or injuring your tarantula.

Disadvantages: Some tarantulas may be shy or fail to detect prey as food. It's also a more complex procedure because you have to manually touch the prey and properly place it within the enclosure.

Free-Range Feeding is releasing the prey into the enclosure and letting the tarantula seek it at its own pace. This strategy is frequently utilized with species that are less shy or have more room in their enclosure to hunt and roam.

Advantages: This method simulates natural hunting behavior, allowing the tarantula to participate in more interesting activities. It also allows the tarantula to feed when it is ready, eliminating the stress of instant engagement with the owner.

Disadvantages: You must guarantee that the prey does not escape, which may result in insects running around your home. Additionally, any uneaten prey should be removed after a few hours to avoid decomposition in the tarantula's enclosure.

Watering your tarantula

In addition to eating, proper hydration is essential for your tarantula's health. While tarantulas can go without food for long periods of time, they require a steady supply of water to sustain their physiological functions and overall health.

Water Dish:

A shallow water dish is the most typical method for keeping your tarantula hydrated. The water dish should be large enough for the tarantula to drink from, but not too deep to keep the spider from drowning.

- Placement: To prevent moisture absorption, place the water dish in a corner of the enclosure away from the substrate. It should be readily available to the tarantula at all times.
- Water Quality: Only use clean, fresh water for your tarantula. Tap water is normally safe, but if you live in a region with hard or chlorinated water, you should drink distilled or filtered water to avoid hazardous minerals and chemicals.

Misting:

While tarantulas acquire the majority of their water from their food, some species, particularly those from more humid locations, may benefit from misting the enclosure on occasion.

- Humidity & spraying: If your tarantula demands more humidity, softly spraying the enclosure with water can assist maintain the appropriate quantity of moisture in the air. However, avoid over-misting, as this can lead to mold growth and other health issues. A light misting once or twice a week is usually sufficient for species that prefer a higher humidity level.

Monitoring Hydration:
It's important to regularly check your tarantula's water dish and replace the water as needed. Tarantulas do not drink a lot of water at once, but they should have access to fresh water at all times.

Feeding your tarantula properly is vital to its overall health, longevity, and well-being. While tarantulas do not require frequent feedings, offering a variety of nutritious prey items and maintaining a healthy feeding schedule will help them thrive. Additionally, proper hydration is equally important, so ensure that your tarantula has access to clean water at all times. By understanding the dietary needs of your tarantula and implementing appropriate feeding techniques, you can ensure that your pet is well-fed, healthy, and content.

Chapter 4

Handling and Interacting with Your Tarantula

Tarantulas are fascinating creatures, but unlike more conventional pets such as cats or dogs, they have very different needs and behaviors. Handling and interacting with a tarantula is a delicate process that requires patience, knowledge, and respect for the spider's nature. While many tarantulas can tolerate handling, it's essential to understand their behavior, body language, and comfort level before interacting with them. In this section, we will explore how to handle a tarantula safely, how to recognize and understand their body language, and how to bond with your tarantula.

How to Handle a Tarantula Safely

Tarantulas are generally not as interactive as mammals, and many species are naturally inclined to avoid human interaction. However, with proper training and knowledge, you can handle your tarantula in a way that is both safe for you and the spider. It's essential to remember that while some tarantulas tolerate handling, others may find it stressful. Always prioritize the spider's well-being, and ensure that you never force interaction when the tarantula is not comfortable.

Understanding When Not to Handle Your Tarantula

Before considering handling, it's essential to know when not to interact with your tarantula:

During Molting: One of the most critical times to avoid handling your tarantula is during its molt. Tarantulas are vulnerable during this period, as they shed their exoskeleton and grow a new one. Handling them during this time can cause serious harm, even death. A tarantula can spend anywhere from a few days to a week molting, and during this time, they will be inactive, hiding in their burrow or retreat.

When Stressed or Hiding: If your tarantula is in its hide or showing signs of stress, such as rapid leg movements or defensive postures, it's best to avoid handling. Stress can be harmful, as it may lead to health problems, including premature molts or even defensive strikes.

When Feeding: Tarantulas are highly focused when hunting or feeding. During this time, they are more likely to be aggressive or defensive. Avoid handling your tarantula when you've just fed it or when it is actively hunting for food.

If the Tarantula Is a Defensive Species: Some species, such as the Mexican redknee or the Chilean rose, are more docile and tolerant of handling, while others, like the Goliath birdeater, can be more defensive. Always research the species you have to determine their general temperament.

The Right Tools for Handling

When handling your tarantula, the first step is to have the proper tools. While some people prefer to use their hands, it is better to use gentle tools that ensure the spider is safely and comfortably moved:

Tongs or Tweezers: Using tongs or forceps is one of the safest ways to move a tarantula. They allow you to gently pick up the tarantula or guide it into a different position without applying direct pressure. Tongs with soft, non-slip tips are ideal, as they minimize the risk of injury to the spider.

Palm of Your Hand: If you're comfortable and your tarantula is calm, you can use the palm of your hand to allow the tarantula to climb onto it. This should be done with great care, and your hand should be placed flat and stable. The tarantula will often climb onto the hand of its own accord if it feels secure.

Plastic Cups or Containers: If you need to move your tarantula from one enclosure to another, use a small plastic cup or container. Gently guide the tarantula into the container using a soft object like a paintbrush or tweezers.

Step-by-Step Guide to Handling

Here is a safe step-by-step guide to handling your tarantula:

Wash Your Hands: Always wash your hands before handling your tarantula. Tarantulas are sensitive to foreign scents or oils that may be left on your skin from lotions, perfumes, or other substances.

Approach Calmly: Move slowly and calmly when approaching your tarantula. Quick movements can startle them, causing stress or defensive reactions.

Use a Gentle Touch: If using your hand, place it flat on the ground and wait for the tarantula to climb onto it. Keep your fingers away from its body and legs as they are sensitive.

Let the Tarantula Move at Its Own Pace: Once the tarantula is in your hand, let it move freely. Do not try to force the tarantula to stay in a specific position. If it wants to climb or move around, let it do so at its own pace.

Avoid Overhandling: Limit handling sessions to short periods. Long handling sessions can stress the tarantula, especially if it becomes tired or frightened. Ten to fifteen-minute interactions are usually sufficient.

Stay Calm: If your tarantula starts to feel threatened or becomes agitated, it may try to run or raise its front legs in a defensive posture. If this happens, calmly place it back in its enclosure. Never drop or let the tarantula fall—always guide it back to safety gently.

Return to the Enclosure: When you are finished, carefully guide the tarantula back into its enclosure. Avoid dropping the spider from any height, as this can lead to injury.

Recognizing and Understanding Body Language

Tarantulas communicate mainly through body language. Unlike mammals, they cannot express emotions verbally or through vocalizations. Understanding their body language is key to ensuring their comfort and safety when interacting with them. Here are some common signs and behaviors to watch for:

Defensive Postures:
When a tarantula feels threatened or stressed, it will display a variety of defensive behaviors. These postures are its way of warning you to stay away, and you should respect these signals to avoid stress or injury.

Upright Position: If a tarantula raises its body off the ground and holds its front legs in the air, it is in a defensive posture. This is a warning that the tarantula feels threatened and may bite if it is provoked further. In this position, the tarantula is trying to appear larger and more intimidating.

Threat Display (Flicking Hairs): Some tarantulas have urticating hairs on their abdomen, which they can flick at perceived threats. These hairs can cause irritation and even injury to human skin or eyes. If your tarantula is flicking its hairs, it's a clear sign that it is agitated and should not be handled.

Hissing or Sound Production: While not common among all species, some tarantulas can produce hissing sounds by rubbing their mouthparts together or by exhaling air through their spiracles. This is another sign of stress or aggression.

Slow, Hesitant Movements: If your tarantula is making slow, cautious movements, it may feel uncertain or uncomfortable in its environment. In these situations, it's best to give the tarantula space and allow it time to adjust.

Calm and Relaxed Behavior:
When your tarantula is calm and comfortable, it will display different behaviors. Recognizing these signs can help you gauge when it's a good time for handling and when it's better to leave it undisturbed.

Normal Crawling or Walking: A calm tarantula will move around its enclosure at a normal pace, either on the ground or up the walls if it's an arboreal species. If the tarantula is exploring and walking without any sudden jerks or rapid movements, it's likely in a relaxed state.

Webbing: Webbing is a sign that the tarantula is feeling secure in its environment. Many species will spin webs to create a retreat or shelter. If your tarantula is actively webbing, it is generally content and not in an immediate defensive state.

Abdomen Position: If the tarantula's abdomen is relaxed and low to the ground, it's often a sign that it's at ease. However, if the abdomen is elevated or puffed out, it may indicate the tarantula is feeling defensive or is preparing to molt.

Molting Behavior:
Molting is a vulnerable and important process for tarantulas. During molting, a tarantula sheds its exoskeleton and grows a new one. The behavior of a tarantula during this time is very different from normal.

Seclusion: Most tarantulas will retreat to a hiding place when they are about to molt. During this time, they become reclusive and are typically less active.

Position During Molt: When molting, the tarantula will lie on its back and remain still for an extended period. It's important not to disturb the tarantula during this time, as it is highly vulnerable.

Post-Molt Behavior: After molting, a tarantula will remain in a defensive state for a few days to weeks until its new exoskeleton hardens. During this time, avoid handling and give the tarantula time to rest and recover.

Bonding with Your Tarantula

Bonding with a tarantula is not the same as bonding with a mammal or bird. Tarantulas are solitary creatures that do not seek affection or companionship in the way that social animals do. However, with time and patience, you can develop a level of trust with your tarantula, making handling and interaction more enjoyable for both you and the spider.

- Patience is Key

Tarantulas do not form bonds in the same way mammals do, and they require time to adjust to their environment and handlers. Some tarantulas may take months or even years to become comfortable with being handled, while others may never tolerate it at all. Always be patient and respect their boundaries.

- Establishing Routine

Establishing a consistent routine for feeding, cleaning, and interaction will help your tarantula feel more comfortable in its environment. A predictable routine provides a sense of security, as the tarantula can learn to anticipate its needs being met without feeling threatened.

- Hand Feeding

If your tarantula is comfortable with handling, you may try hand-feeding it with tongs or tweezers. This type of interaction can help build trust between you and the tarantula. Start by feeding the tarantula from a distance and gradually move the food closer to it over time.

- Observing and Admiring

Even if your tarantula does not enjoy handling, you can still bond by observing and admiring its natural behaviors. Spending time watching your tarantula build webs, hunt, or simply move around its enclosure allows you to connect with the creature in a more passive way.

Handling and interacting with your tarantula can be a rewarding experience, but it requires care, patience, and respect for the spider's nature. By understanding the proper techniques for handling, reading and responding to the tarantula's body language, and fostering a comfortable and safe environment, you can create a positive relationship with your pet tarantula. Always prioritize the well-being of your tarantula, and remember that not all species or individuals will enjoy handling it. With patience, you can develop a healthy and respectful relationship with your tarantula, fostering a bond built on mutual trust and understanding.

Chapter 5

Health and Wellness of Your Tarantula

Tarantulas are fascinating creatures, but like all pets, they require attention and care to ensure their well-being. While tarantulas are generally hardy creatures, they can still experience health issues if not provided with the proper care, environment, or nutrition. It's essential to recognize the signs of a healthy tarantula and be aware of common health issues so you can address them early. Additionally, understanding the process of molting and how to support your tarantula during shedding is crucial for their overall health and wellness.

Signs of a Healthy Tarantula

Understanding what constitutes a healthy tarantula is essential for every tarantula owner. Healthy tarantulas typically display specific behaviors, physical characteristics, and overall activity that indicate their well-being. Here are the key signs to look for in a healthy tarantula:

- Physical Appearance

Clean and Smooth Exoskeleton: A healthy tarantula will have a clean, smooth, and intact exoskeleton. It should not have any cracks, tears, or discolorations on its outer shell. A tarantula with visible damage to its exoskeleton, such as cracks or missing legs, may have experienced a traumatic injury or health problem.

- Full Abdomen: A healthy tarantula should have a rounded, firm abdomen. It should not appear overly thin, emaciated, or excessively bloated. An overly thin abdomen can indicate malnutrition or dehydration, while a bloated abdomen might suggest issues like overfeeding or internal parasites.
- Normal Leg Movement: Healthy tarantulas move their legs smoothly and evenly. Each leg should have normal mobility, and the tarantula should be able to walk and climb with ease. A tarantula that struggles to move its legs or appears immobile might be experiencing a neurological issue or injury.

Bright, Clear Eyes: While tarantulas have relatively poor eyesight, they do rely on their vision to detect movement and perceive their environment. Healthy tarantulas will have bright, clear eyes.

Cloudy, sunken, or discolored eyes might indicate illness or dehydration.

Coloration: Healthy tarantulas usually display vibrant and natural colors. The coloration may vary depending on the species, but a dull or faded color could be a sign of stress, dehydration, or malnutrition. Pay attention to any unusual discoloration, as it could be indicative of a health issue.

- Behavior and Activity

Normal Behavior: A healthy tarantula is usually active, exploring its enclosure, or creating webs. While some tarantulas may prefer to remain hidden, they should still be alert and move around from time to time. A tarantula that is constantly lethargic, inactive, or hiding without any movement for extended periods may be ill.

Healthy Appetite: A healthy tarantula will have a good appetite and actively hunt or scavenge for food. When you offer prey, the tarantula should show interest and be able to capture and consume it. A lack of appetite or refusal to eat for an extended period could signal a health issue, such as stress, molting, or illness.

Molting Behavior: Molting is an essential process for tarantulas, and a healthy tarantula will molt regularly, typically every 6–12 months depending on age, species, and environmental factors. During this time, the tarantula will hide and remain inactive. If your tarantula is preparing to molt, it will exhibit specific behaviors, such as secluding itself and becoming more reclusive. Molting is a natural process, but if the tarantula seems to struggle or fail to complete the molt, it may be a sign of health problems.

- Regularly Inspecting Your Tarantula

It's important to regularly inspect your tarantula to ensure its health. When handling or observing your tarantula, gently check its legs, body, and eyes. This allows you to detect early signs of health issues and address them before they become more serious.

Common Health Issues and Their Solutions

While tarantulas are generally hardy, they can encounter health problems due to environmental stressors, poor nutrition, or underlying conditions. Below are some common health issues that tarantula owners may encounter, along with their solutions:

1. Dehydration

Tarantulas can easily become dehydrated if they do not have access to clean water or if their environment lacks proper humidity levels. Dehydration can lead to lethargy, loss of appetite, and even death if not addressed.

Signs of Dehydration:

- A shrunken or shriveled abdomen.
- Lethargy and a lack of movement.
- Refusal to eat or drink.
- Difficulty molting or incomplete molts.

Solution: To address dehydration, ensure that your tarantula has a fresh, clean water dish available at all times. Mist the enclosure lightly if the species requires higher humidity levels. Additionally, check the temperature and humidity in the tank to ensure that they are within the appropriate range for your tarantula species.

2. Mite Infestation

Tarantulas are susceptible to mite infestations, which can affect their health. These microscopic parasites feed on the tarantula's blood and can cause stress, skin irritation, and even death if left untreated.

Signs of Mites:

- Small, white, or red specks moving on the tarantula's body or in the substrate.
- Skin irritation or sores on the tarantula's exoskeleton.
- Excessive grooming or scratching by the tarantula.

Solution: To treat a mite infestation, isolate the affected tarantula from other pets to prevent the mites from spreading. Carefully remove the tarantula from its enclosure and clean the entire habitat thoroughly, discarding any contaminated substrate. Use a mild solution of insecticidal soap or neem oil (safe for tarantulas) to treat the mites. If the infestation is severe, consider using a mite treatment specifically designed for arachnids.

3. Mold or Fungal Growth

Tarantulas are susceptible to mold and fungal growth in their enclosures, particularly in humid environments. Mold can grow on uneaten food, wet substrate, or stagnant water. Mold exposure can cause respiratory issues and weaken the tarantula's immune system.

Signs of Mold or Fungal Growth:

- Visible mold or fungus on the substrate or decorations.
- White or grayish fuzz growing on uneaten food or organic matter.
- Respiratory distress in the tarantula (increased movements, open mouth, or sluggishness).

Solution: To combat mold and fungal growth, remove any uneaten food from the enclosure promptly, as it can quickly decompose and create a breeding ground for mold. Ensure the enclosure is properly ventilated to reduce excess moisture and humidity. If mold is present, remove the affected substrate, clean the enclosure thoroughly, and replace the substrate with fresh, dry material.

4. Obesity

Although tarantulas do not overeat as easily as other pets, excessive feeding can lead to obesity, particularly if they are fed too frequently or with food that is too large for their size. Obesity can shorten the lifespan of a tarantula and lead to various health problems, including difficulty molting.

Signs of Obesity:

- A visibly enlarged or bloated abdomen.
- Lack of movement or activity.
- Difficulty in molting (e.g., incomplete molts or failure to molt).

Solution: To prevent obesity, feed your tarantula appropriately-sized prey based on its species, size, and age. Generally, adult tarantulas should be fed once every 1–2 weeks, while younger tarantulas may need more frequent feedings. Ensure that the tarantula's diet consists of live insects like crickets, roaches, or mealworms, and avoid overfeeding or offering prey that is too large.

5. Leg Injury or Loss

Tarantulas have the ability to regenerate lost legs, but if an injury occurs, it can be a significant stressor for the tarantula. Leg injuries can happen during handling, falls, or interactions with prey. Although tarantulas can regenerate lost legs over time, it's important to monitor the injury to prevent infection.

Signs of Leg Injury:

- Missing or damaged legs.

- A limp or abnormal gait when walking.
- Open wounds or signs of infection around the injury.

Solution: If your tarantula has a leg injury, isolate it from potential stressors or other pets. Clean the wound with a mild saline solution to reduce the risk of infection. In many cases, the tarantula will naturally regenerate its missing limb after a successful molt. However, if there is severe damage or infection, it is best to consult an experienced veterinarian who specializes in exotic pets.

6. Parasites and Internal Issues

Internal parasites, such as nematodes or protozoans, can cause digestive problems or general weakness in tarantulas. Parasites are often contracted from contaminated food or water and can lead to significant health problems if not treated.

Signs of Parasites:

- Loss of appetite and weight loss.
- Lethargy or weakness.
- Abnormal excrement (liquid, unusually dark, or containing visible worms).

Solution: If you suspect internal parasites, it's important to consult with an exotic pet veterinarian who can diagnose and treat the problem. Treatment may involve medication designed to treat parasitic infections in tarantulas. To prevent future issues, ensure that your tarantula is fed clean, properly sourced food and that its water is fresh and uncontaminated.

Dealing with Molting and Shedding

Molting is a natural and essential process for tarantulas as they grow. During a molt, the tarantula sheds its old exoskeleton and replaces it with a new, larger one. This process can be stressful and requires careful attention to ensure the tarantula remains healthy throughout the molt. It's important to understand how to properly care for your tarantula during this period to prevent complications.

The Molting Process

Molting occurs in several stages:

Pre-Molt Stage: During this stage, the tarantula may become reclusive, stop eating, and seek out a safe, quiet place to molt. It will often stop moving around and may exhibit signs of lethargy.

The tarantula will also begin to soften its exoskeleton in preparation for the molt.

Molting Stage: The molting process itself involves the tarantula shedding its old exoskeleton. This can take anywhere from a few hours to a full day, depending on the species and size of the tarantula. The tarantula will lie on its back and begin to pull its exoskeleton off in pieces, starting with the legs and working its way toward the body.

Post-Molt Stage: After the molt, the tarantula will be soft and vulnerable. It may take several days to a few weeks for the new exoskeleton to harden and become fully functional. During this period, the tarantula will be more sluggish and should not be handled or disturbed.

Supporting Your Tarantula During Molting

Provide a Quiet Environment: During the molt, provide your tarantula with a quiet and undisturbed environment. Avoid handling it, as this could cause stress and interfere with the molt.

Maintain Proper Humidity: Humidity plays a crucial role during molting. Ensure the enclosure is maintained at the correct humidity levels, as dry conditions can lead to incomplete molts, which may result in health problems.

Do Not Disturb: Avoid disturbing the tarantula during the molt. If the tarantula is struggling or appears to be having trouble, do not try to assist it unless you have experience and knowledge in handling molting tarantulas.

Post-Molt Care: After the molt, allow the tarantula time to rest and recover. Provide it with easy access to water, as it may be dehydrated. Avoid offering food until the exoskeleton has hardened.

Maintaining the health and wellness of your tarantula requires careful attention to their environment, diet, and behaviors. Understanding the signs of a healthy tarantula, recognizing common health issues, and knowing how to support your tarantula during molting are essential aspects of tarantula care. Regular observation, proper nutrition, and a clean and safe habitat are the cornerstones of ensuring your tarantula lives a long and healthy life. By being proactive about health issues and providing your tarantula with the proper care, you can ensure its well-being and enjoy a fulfilling relationship with your fascinating pet.

Chapter 6

Breeding and Reproduction of Tarantulas

Tarantulas, like all arachnids, have an intriguing and complex reproductive process that is as captivating as the creatures themselves. While most tarantula enthusiasts are content to keep these spiders as pets, many also find themselves fascinated by the idea of breeding them. Understanding the basics of tarantula reproduction, as well as how to raise baby tarantulas (spiderlings), is an essential step for those looking to breed their tarantulas or simply deepen their knowledge of these fascinating creatures.

The Basics of Tarantula Reproduction

Before attempting to breed tarantulas, it's important to first understand the biology and reproductive behavior of these spiders. Reproduction in tarantulas is a fascinating and sometimes complex process, involving courtship rituals, mating behavior, and post-mating care.

- Tarantula Sexual Dimorphism

Tarantulas, like many other animals, display sexual dimorphism, meaning that males and females differ in size, coloration, and sometimes behavior. Female tarantulas are generally larger and more robust than males. The size difference plays a significant role in the reproductive process, as the male must approach the female carefully to avoid being eaten. This phenomenon is often seen in many species of tarantulas, where males have evolved specialized behaviors to court females while minimizing the risk of predation.

Females are typically the more dominant sex in tarantula species. They can live much longer than males, sometimes up to 25 years, and are the ones that produce eggs. Female tarantulas are often territorial and can become aggressive toward males if not properly courted.

Males are smaller and have evolved specific behaviors to attract females. Males are usually only alive for a few years (often around 2–5 years), and their sole purpose is to mate. They often develop specialized structures, such as tibial spurs or pedipalps, which help them with mating.

- Mating Behavior and Courtship

Mating in tarantulas is a delicate and ritualistic process. The courtship and mating process can vary depending on the species, but it generally follows a similar pattern across the board:

Approaching the Female: Male tarantulas typically approach a female by tapping their pedipalps (small leg-like appendages near the mouth) on the ground, creating a vibrating signal that may attract the female. The male may also perform a "dance" or specific movements, such as raising his front legs and tapping or drumming on the female's web or enclosure. These movements serve to communicate his presence and intentions. If the female is receptive, she will respond by lifting her legs, which signals her willingness to mate.

Copulation: If the female is receptive to the male's advances, copulation will occur. The male will use his pedipalps to transfer sperm to the female's spermatheca, the sperm storage organs. The process can be quick, lasting anywhere from a few minutes to an hour, depending on the species.

Risks for Males: Male tarantulas are at risk during copulation, as some species have females that are aggressive toward males. In some instances, the female may attack and eat the male after mating. This behavior is more common in certain species like the Haplopelma and Grammostola genera, where males must tread carefully to avoid being consumed. The male's strategy is often to mate as quickly as possible, sometimes fleeing the female immediately after copulation to avoid being eaten.

- Female Egg Production

Once mating has occurred, the female will fertilize her eggs internally, and the eggs will be stored in her spermatheca for several months before being laid. The timing of egg-laying depends on environmental factors such as temperature, humidity, and food availability.

Female tarantulas will typically produce an egg sac after mating. The egg sac contains hundreds or even thousands of fertilized eggs. The female will wrap the eggs in silk and protect the sac until the spiderlings hatch. The number of eggs varies depending on the species; smaller species may produce a few hundred eggs, while larger species can lay thousands.

- Egg Sac and Incubation

Egg Sac: The egg sac is created by the female using her spinnerets, which secrete silk. She will place the egg sac in a secure location, often in a burrow or hidden away in a corner of the enclosure, to keep it safe from predators or environmental threats. The female will guard the egg sac vigilantly, rarely leaving it unattended.

Incubation: The incubation period for tarantula eggs typically lasts between 6 to 10 weeks, depending on the species and environmental conditions. During this time, the female does not usually eat, focusing solely on guarding the egg sac. The temperature and humidity levels are crucial during this stage, as extreme conditions can affect the development of the eggs.

Raising Baby Tarantulas (Spiderlings)

After the incubation period, the egg sac will hatch, and the baby tarantulas, known as spiderlings, will emerge. Raising tarantula spiderlings can be a rewarding yet challenging experience, as these tiny creatures require special care and attention. While tarantula babies are independent from birth, they still need a safe environment to grow and thrive.

- Spiderling Emergence and First Molt

When the egg sac hatches, hundreds of tiny spiderlings will emerge. At this stage, they are extremely small (often only a few millimeters in length) and fragile. Most spiderlings are capable of independent movement and will start exploring their environment in search of food. However, they will not eat immediately after hatching and will undergo their first molt (instar) within a few days.

First Molt: The first molt is crucial for the survival of spiderlings. During this molt, they shed their exoskeleton and develop a larger, more robust body. This process allows them to grow and better survive in their environment. The first molt can take anywhere from a few days to a week after hatching, depending on factors like temperature and humidity.

Separation from the Mother: Once the spiderlings have undergone their first molt, they become fully independent and begin hunting for their own food. The mother may continue to guard the egg sac for a while, but eventually, she will abandon it. At this point, the spiderlings are ready to be separated from the mother and raised independently.

- Housing and Care for Spiderlings

Raising tarantula spiderlings requires careful attention to their environment. Spiderlings are extremely small and delicate, so the setup must be appropriate for their size and needs. Here are some key considerations for raising healthy tarantula spiderlings:

Housing: Unlike adult tarantulas, which often require larger enclosures, spiderlings can live in small containers, such as plastic vials, small jars, or delicup containers. These small enclosures should have adequate ventilation to prevent moisture buildup and mold growth. The size of the container should be just enough for the spiderling to move around comfortably and hide if it feels threatened.

Substrate: Spiderlings do not need deep substrate, as they are still small and delicate. A shallow layer of moist soil or coconut fiber will provide enough moisture for hydration. It's important to maintain proper humidity levels without over-wetting the substrate, as excess moisture can lead to mold and other issues.

Temperature and Humidity: Like adults, spiderlings require a warm and humid environment to thrive. The temperature should be kept within the optimal range for the species, usually between 75–85°F (24–29°C). Humidity levels should be carefully monitored and maintained within the ideal range for the species. Some species, like the Brachypelma genus, require lower humidity, while others, like Chromatopelma species, thrive in more humid conditions.

Feeding: Spiderlings need small prey items, such as fruit flies, pinhead crickets, or small mealworms. Offer them live prey, as they will hunt for food in their environment. It's crucial not to overfeed spiderlings, as they can become overweight or develop issues from consuming prey that is too large. Feed spiderlings every 2–3 days, ensuring that any uneaten food is removed after 24 hours.

- Molting and Growth

As spiderlings grow, they will molt several times before reaching adulthood. Each molt is critical for their development, as it allows them to increase in size and strength. Molting is a delicate process, and it's essential to provide an environment that supports the spiderling's ability to molt successfully.

Signs of Molting: Before molting, spiderlings may become less active, refuse food, or hide away in a secure spot. They will also appear to have a cloudy or milky appearance to their exoskeleton as the new exoskeleton develops beneath the old one. It's important not to disturb the spiderling during this time, as it can cause stress and hinder the molting process.

Post-Molt Care: After molting, spiderlings need time to harden their new exoskeleton. This process can take several days, during which time they should not be handled or fed. Once their exoskeleton has hardened, they can resume normal activities, including eating.

- Reaching Juvenile Stage

After several molts, spiderlings will grow into juvenile tarantulas. Juveniles are more robust and capable of handling a wider variety of food. At this stage, the tarantula is more independent and can be moved into larger enclosures suitable for its growing size.

Breeding and raising tarantulas can be a fascinating and rewarding experience, but it requires patience, attention to detail, and a deep understanding of the reproductive process and spiderling care. By understanding the basics of tarantula reproduction and creating the right environment for your spiderlings, you can ensure their health and success as they grow from tiny, delicate creatures into full-grown adults.

Tarantula breeding is a commitment that involves ensuring the safety and well-being of both the adults and the young spiders. By providing the right conditions, proper nutrition, and a safe environment for molting, breeders can successfully raise healthy tarantulas and contribute to the continuation of these incredible arachnids.

Chapter 7

Safety and Precautions: Handling Venomous Tarantulas

Tarantulas, though often feared due to their size and reputation, are generally not as dangerous as many believe. With their somewhat docile nature, tarantulas are typically low-risk animals when it comes to human interaction, especially when the proper precautions are taken. However, like any exotic pet, tarantulas do pose certain risks, particularly venomous species, and understanding these risks, myths, and proper safety precautions is essential for both the pet owner and the tarantula.

Handling Venomous Tarantulas: Myths and Facts
Venomous tarantulas are often perceived as more dangerous than they actually are. Most of these spiders are not aggressive toward humans and will only bite if they feel threatened or cornered. Despite this, many myths surrounding tarantula venom and bites persist. It is important to understand the nature of

venomous species and separate fact from fiction to handle them safely.

What Makes a Tarantula Venomous?

All tarantulas possess venom, which is used to subdue their prey in the wild. Tarantula venom is primarily designed to immobilize small prey items, such as insects and other arthropods, and to begin the digestive process. However, tarantula venom is typically not harmful to humans. In most cases, a bite may cause mild symptoms such as pain, redness, or swelling, which usually subside after a few hours or days.

The venomous species of tarantulas that are of primary concern to humans are those whose venom is potent enough to cause noticeable effects beyond mild irritation. These species are generally more defensive and may bite if they feel threatened. However, even with these species, the venom is rarely life-threatening.

Venomous Species: Some of the more venomous species of tarantulas include:

- Poecilotheria species (Pokie Tarantulas): Known for their defensive nature, these species are venomous and can cause significant pain and swelling with a bite.
- Haplopelma species: These species are more aggressive, and their venom can cause moderate to severe pain.
- Theraphosa blondi (Goliath Birdeater): Although large and intimidating, the Goliath Birdeater's venom is not typically dangerous to humans, though it can still cause localized pain.

Non-Venomous Species: While most species of tarantulas have venom, many are not considered dangerous to humans. The venom of these species is typically too mild to cause more than a localized reaction. Some examples include:

- Brachypelma species (Mexican Redknee Tarantula): Known for being docile and non-aggressive, their venom is relatively harmless to humans.
- Grammostola species (Chilean Rose Tarantula): These tarantulas are slow-moving and known for their calm temperament. Their venom poses little risk to humans.

Myths About Venomous Tarantulas

There are many myths surrounding venomous tarantulas that often lead to unnecessary fear or misunderstanding of their nature. It is essential to debunk these myths to provide proper education and promote safe handling practices.

Myth: All Tarantulas Are Dangerous to Humans Fact: Not all tarantulas are dangerous. The majority of tarantulas are not aggressive and their venom is relatively harmless to humans. Bites from even the most venomous species typically result in no more than temporary pain and swelling.

Myth: Venomous Tarantulas Can Kill a Human Fact: While tarantula venom can cause localized symptoms such as pain, swelling, and in some cases, nausea or dizziness, it is very unlikely that a tarantula bite would be fatal to a healthy adult human. Even in cases where a venomous tarantula bites, the effects are generally not life-threatening.

Myth: Tarantula Bites Are Always Extremely Painful Fact: The pain from a tarantula bite varies depending on the species and individual response. While some venomous species may cause moderate pain, many people report that the bite feels similar to a bee sting, with some only experiencing mild irritation. The pain typically subsides within a few hours.

Myth: Tarantulas Will Seek Out Humans to Bite Fact: Tarantulas do not seek out humans to bite. They are generally docile creatures and will only bite in self-defense when they feel threatened, cornered, or provoked. Most tarantulas will try to escape rather than confront a threat.

Avoiding Bites and Other Risks

While tarantulas are not inherently dangerous, it is still important to take precautions when handling them to avoid bites and other potential risks. Even though tarantulas are often shy creatures that prefer to avoid human contact, it is important to understand their behavior and respond accordingly.

Recognizing When a Tarantula Feels Threatened

Tarantulas give clear signs when they feel threatened or are preparing to defend themselves. Recognizing these signs can help you avoid provoking a bite.

Threat Display: When a tarantula feels threatened, it may rear up on its hind legs and display its fangs in a defensive posture. This is a clear warning sign that the tarantula feels cornered and is preparing to defend itself. If you see your tarantula doing this, it's important to back off and give it space.

Hissing or Tapping: Some tarantulas will make noise by hissing or tapping their fangs or legs when threatened. This is another warning sign to stop and reassess the situation. Species like the Theraphosa blondi (Goliath Birdeater) may even make sounds by rubbing their legs together in an attempt to scare off predators.

Raising Front Legs: Many tarantulas will raise their front legs and spread their fangs when threatened. This is an intimidation tactic designed to make the tarantula appear larger. If your tarantula exhibits this behavior, it is important to avoid any sudden movements or attempts at handling.

Hair Flicking: Some species, like Psalmopoeus or Lasiodora species, can flick urticating hairs from their abdomen when threatened. These hairs are irritating to the skin and eyes and can cause discomfort or even allergic reactions. Always be cautious of this behavior, especially when handling or cleaning enclosures.

- Proper Handling Techniques

If you decide to handle your tarantula, proper handling techniques can reduce the risk of bites and stress for both you and your pet.

Slow Movements: When handling a tarantula, always move slowly and deliberately. Sudden movements can startle the tarantula and provoke a defensive reaction. Allow the tarantula to move freely onto your hand if it feels comfortable.

Use a Holding Container: If you're unsure whether your tarantula is calm enough for handling, use a shallow holding container to coax it out rather than directly handling it. You can gently guide the tarantula onto your hand or a flat surface using a soft paintbrush.

Avoid Handling After a Molt: Never handle your tarantula immediately after it has molted. During this time, the tarantula's exoskeleton is soft, and it is extremely vulnerable. Handling it could cause injury, and the stress of handling may interfere with the molting process.

Support Its Body: Always support the tarantula's body when handling it. This is especially important with larger species, as their legs are fragile and could easily be injured if not properly supported.

Keep Hands Clean: Make sure your hands are clean and free of any chemicals, lotions, or oils before handling your tarantula. Tarantulas are sensitive to changes in their environment, and chemicals on your skin could harm them.

- What to Do in Case of a Bite

Though bites from tarantulas are rare and usually harmless, it's important to know how to respond if you are bitten.

Stay Calm: The first and most important step is to remain calm. Tarantula bites are rarely life-threatening, and the pain is usually mild. Panicking will only make the situation worse and may cause unnecessary stress.

Clean the Wound: After a bite, clean the wound with soap and water to reduce the risk of infection. Apply a cold compress to the bite site to reduce swelling and pain.

Monitor for Reactions: Most tarantula bites result in no more than a slight stinging sensation, localized swelling, and redness.

However, if you experience significant swelling, dizziness, nausea, or difficulty breathing, seek medical attention immediately.

Seek Medical Attention: In rare cases, people may experience more severe reactions to a tarantula bite, particularly if they are allergic to the venom. If symptoms persist or worsen, it's crucial to seek medical help. Some species of tarantulas may cause more intense reactions due to their venom potency, and professional medical intervention is required.

- General Safety Precautions

Educate Yourself: Before acquiring a tarantula, make sure you understand the species' temperament and potential risks. Some tarantulas are more defensive than others, and it's important to choose a species that matches your experience level and comfort with handling them.

Safe Housing: Keep your tarantula in a secure enclosure with a proper lid. Tarantulas are excellent escape artists, and an unsecured enclosure can lead to an escape. An escapee can cause unnecessary stress, and in some cases, the tarantula may end up getting injured or lost.

Avoid Handling When Sick or on Medication: If you're feeling unwell or on medication that could affect your coordination or judgment, avoid handling your tarantula. A lack of concentration or sudden movements could lead to a bite or injury to the spider.

Children and Pets: Keep tarantulas out of reach of children and pets. Even though tarantulas are typically not aggressive, it's always best to supervise interactions to ensure no harm comes to either the tarantula or the humans and animals involved.

Handling tarantulas, including venomous species, can be a safe and enjoyable experience when done with the proper precautions. It's important to understand the myths surrounding tarantula venom and bites, recognize the signs of a threatened spider, and follow safe handling techniques. By doing so, you can avoid bites and other risks associated with these incredible creatures. Tarantulas, while commonly feared, are generally docile and non-aggressive when handled with care. You can have a safe and happy connection with these interesting arachnids by keeping them in a secure habitat, learning their behaviors, and handling them with care.

Chapter 8

Common Misconceptions and Myths about Tarantulas

By addressing prevalent misconceptions and refuting preconceptions about tarantulas, we can gain a better understanding of their position in the environment, behavior, and distinguishing traits. This article seeks to provide clarification, dispel myths, and showcase the amazing and fascinating facts about tarantulas.

Dispelling Fears and Misconceptions

Tarantulas are frequently feared for their size, look, and reputation in popular culture, however many of these anxieties are unwarranted. Understanding the facts of keeping a tarantula as a pet can help to reduce the stigma and promote careful ownership.

Myth 1: All tarantulas are dangerous to humans.

One of the most widely held beliefs about tarantulas is that all kinds are hazardous to humans. While tarantulas do carry venom, the great majority of species' venom is harmless to humans. In truth, most tarantulas' venom is barely strong enough to immobilize their victims, which are usually small insects or other invertebrates.

Tarantula bites sometimes occur, although they are uncommon and usually cause little harm to humans. The venom of most species causes only mild irritation, similar to a bee sting or a slight allergic reaction. Only a few species, such as Poecilotheria and Haplopelma, produce venom that can cause substantial pain or swelling in humans. However, these bites are rarely fatal.

Myth 2: Tarantulas are aggressive and will attack humans.

Another prevalent misconception is that tarantulas are hostile and intentionally seek out humans to attack. This misperception is most likely based on their menacing look, which includes big teeth and a formidable bulk. Tarantulas, on the other hand, are typically solitary and defensive creatures.

Tarantulas are not typically aggressive toward people. In fact, most tarantulas will avoid human contact if given the chance. They will only bite when they feel threatened or cornered. Even the most protective animals may frequently demonstrate warning behaviors, such as rising up on their hind legs or elevating their front legs in a menacing stance, rather than instantly attacking.

Tarantulas are generally calm creatures which prefer to live in their burrows or hide under rocks and logs in the wild. When confined in a suitable habitat, pet tarantulas exhibit comparable habits, and they normally only become aggressive when provoked or feel unsafe.

Myth 3: Tarantulas can run faster than humans.

Tarantulas are often said to be able to outrun humans, which undoubtedly contributes to their fearsome reputation. Tarantulas are faster than most other spiders, but not fast enough to outrun a human.

Tarantulas are relatively swift for their size, but this is not cause for fear. Tarantulas typically move at speeds of 1-2 feet per second, which is rapid for a spider but far too slow to outrun a human. Their primary form of defense is not speed, but rather the capacity to intimidate, burrow, or retreat to safety.

Tarantulas move slowly, especially when they are old or in captivity. They do not pursue prey, but rather rely on ambushes or patiently waiting for food to come to them.

Myth 4: Tarantulas are poisonous, not just venomous.

The phrases "poisonous" and "venomous" are sometimes confused, yet they have distinct meanings. Poisonous refers to a material that might cause harm when consumed, whereas venomous refers to a substance delivered via bite or sting.

Tarantulas are venomous but not poisonous. Their venom is mostly employed to sedate animals in the wild, however it is generally safe for humans. As previously said, bites can cause moderate symptoms such as pain, redness, and swelling, but they are not life-threatening. Tarantulas do not produce poisons that are harmful to humans if swallowed, and their venom is only effective when injected through their fangs.

Myth 5: Tarantulas can only live a few months.

Tarantulas are commonly thought to have limited lifespans, which is due to their small size and slow movement. Many tarantulas, particularly females, live far longer than expected.

Tarantulas can live for several years, depending on the species, and females frequently outlive males by a large margin. Some tarantulas, including the Brachypelma species (e.g., Mexican Redknee), can survive in captivity for more than 20 years. Males often survive only a few years because their major purpose is reproduction. Females, on the other hand, can live for far longer due to their slower development rate and reduced biological demands.

While tarantula lifespans vary by species, pet tarantulas can live for 10 years or more, making them relatively long-lived pets when compared to other small animals.

Myth 6: Tarantulas are dirty and dangerous to have as pets.

Some people assume that tarantulas are difficult to care for and make unsanitary, dangerous pets. This belief is supported by misconceptions about their natural routines and demands.

Tarantulas are low-maintenance pets that aren't naturally dirty. Tarantulas are frequently found in burrows or other protected habitats in the wild, where they remain hidden from view. In captivity, their habitats can be maintained clean by doing routine maintenance such as removing uneaten food, cleaning their water dish, and spot-cleaning any excrement. Tarantulas do not require much handling and do not produce significant scents.

Their food is mostly insect-based, making them clean eaters, and they are also quite good at managing their waste. Tarantulas are relatively sanitary when housed in a well-maintained enclosure with the proper substrate and represent no additional risk to pet owners.

Interesting facts about tarantulas

Aside from myths and misconceptions, tarantulas are actually intriguing creatures. Here are some fascinating facts about tarantulas that may change your perspective on these amazing arachnids.

1. Tarantulas have unique defense mechanisms.

Tarantulas are not defenseless; they have several distinct defense mechanisms to protect themselves from predators. One of the most fascinating is their ability to flick urticating hairs out of their abdomen. These small, barbed hairs can irritate the skin and eyes of prospective predators, including other animals and humans.

Some species, such as those in the Psalmopoeus and Lasiodora genera, are very adept at flicking their urticating hairs when threatened. These hairs can inflict severe itching, redness, and discomfort, discouraging predators from attacking.

In addition to flicking hairs, many tarantulas can hide in tunnels or under rocks to escape encounters with larger creatures.

2. Tarantulas can regrow limbs.

Tarantulas have the remarkable capacity to regenerate lost limbs, which is more prevalent among arthropods than vertebrates. If a tarantula loses a leg due to injury, it can grow a new one after several molts. This technique, known as "autotomy," allows the spider to heal from injury and function normally in the wild or in captivity.

However, the regrown limb is not always as flawless as the original. It may be smaller or less useful, but it permits the tarantula to remain mobile and hunt. Tarantulas rely on their capacity to survive in a world full of predators and accidents.

3. Tarantulas have a slower metabolism.

Tarantulas are not high-energy animals and have a slower metabolism than most other animals. They may go for lengthy periods of time without eating due to their poor metabolism. In reality, many tarantula species can go for weeks or even months without eating, especially during periods of fasting like molting.

Tarantulas are one of the most successful predators due to their slow metabolism and efficient energy utilization. They do not require continual eating and frequently rely on ambushing their victim or waiting for food to come to them.

4. Tarantulas can survive for decades.

While male tarantulas may only live a few years, many female tarantula species can live for decades, making them surprisingly long-lived pets. Some tarantulas, such the Brachypelma and Grammostola species, can survive for up to 30 years in captivity.

Tarantulas are excellent pets for dedicated enthusiasts due to their long longevity. Tarantulas, unlike some small animals with brief lifespans, provide years of companionship and intrigue.

5. Tarantulas "hear" through their legs.

Tarantulas do not have ears like mammals, but they are extremely sensitive to vibrations and can "hear" via unique sensory organs on their legs. These organs, known as "setae," respond to vibrations in the air and ground, allowing the tarantula to sense potential dangers or prey.

Tarantulas' capacity to detect vibrations aids them in navigating their environment, particularly in the dark, and allows them to locate prey without the use of traditional vision. Their sensitivity to vibrations enables them to notice the movements of possible predators, which is crucial for survival.

Tarantulas are frequently misunderstood creatures, and many of the anxieties associated with them stem from misconceptions and myths. By refuting these beliefs and presenting the amazing facts about these remarkable spiders, we can gain a better understanding of them and their place in nature.

Tarantulas are not the scary, aggressive creatures that they are frequently depicted to be. Instead, they are mostly quiet, low-maintenance pets who can live for many years and have a variety of amazing features. Tarantulas are very rare and interesting creatures, with their capacity to regenerate severed limbs and highly sensitive legs that allow them to "hear."

Understanding tarantulas better would help to eliminate the fear and ignorance surrounding them, as well as build a stronger appreciation for these extraordinary arachnids. Whether you're a seasoned spider aficionado or fresh to the world of tarantulas, there's a lot to learn and enjoy about these incredible creatures.

Conclusion

The Benefits of Tarantula Ownership

Owning a tarantula may be an extremely gratifying experience for any pet lover. While these interesting creatures may appear daunting at first, they quickly prove to be distinct, captivating, and low-maintenance friends. Tarantulas can live for many years with the proper care and understanding, and their owners will feel a deep feeling of fulfillment and admiration for the world of arachnids.

In this section, we'll look at why tarantulas are such interesting pets, as well as the main advantages of owning one. In addition, we will provide some last long-term care suggestions to assist ensure that your tarantula flourishes in its surroundings, giving you years of delight and company.

Why Tarantulas Make Interesting Pets?

Tarantulas are not the most common pet choice, but they are unquestionably one of the most interesting and distinctive critters you may own. There are numerous reasons why these spiders may be such interesting additions to your home.

1. Low maintenance.

Tarantulas are one of the easiest pets to care for. Unlike dogs, cats, and even certain reptiles, tarantulas do not require continual attention or feeding. Their slow metabolism allows them to go extended periods without feeding, and their enclosures only require occasional cleaning and maintenance.

Tarantulas are also solitary animals, therefore they don't require social connection or continual stimulation. This makes them perfect pets for folks who lead busy lives or who want a companion that does not require a lot of their time. If you work full-time or have limited room, a tarantula is a great option.

Their diet is likewise basic and cheap. Tarantulas are primarily carnivorous, eating on living insects including crickets, mealworms, and roaches. These insects are simple to purchase and care for, allowing tarantula owners to supply them with a steady food source. Furthermore, because tarantulas eat seldom, feeding them once or twice each week is generally adequate.

2. Fascinating Behavior and Movement

Tarantulas are fascinating to witness since they exhibit a variety of unusual behaviors that will attract any animal lover. Their slow, deliberate motions are captivating, particularly when hunting or exploring their enclosure. Watching a tarantula in motion may be both relaxing and enlightening, providing insight into the complex and frequently hidden world of arachnids.

Tarantulas have unique hunting tactics, such as patiently waiting for prey to approach or stalking food before pouncing. Many species, including those in the Poecilotheria and Brachypelma genera, are arboreal and spend a large amount of time climbing, which adds to the mystery of their behavior. Ground-dwelling organisms can be observed digging burrows or tunneling through substrate, emulating their natural home and exhibiting their adaptability to many settings.

Tarantulas also have a remarkable molting process. Tarantulas must shed their exoskeleton as they grow, which is referred to as ecdysis. This happens multiple times in their life, and it's a thrilling experience to observe. The tarantula removes its old skin to show a new, bigger exoskeleton beneath. While molting can be a dangerous time for tarantulas, it is a distinct feature of their life cycle that adds to the allure of having one.

3. Colors and species diversity

Another reason tarantulas make such interesting pets is the sheer number of kinds available. Tarantulas come in over 1,000 different species, ranging from little to huge, friendly to defensive, and in a variety of colors and patterns. Whether you prefer brilliant colors like the magnificent blue of the Chromatopelma cyaneopubescens or more subtle earth tones like the Grammostola rosea, there is a tarantula to suit you.

Tarantulas' colors and patterns can be beautiful. Some species have vivid orange, red, or yellow markings on their legs and abdomen, while others have intricate patterns that help them blend in with their natural surroundings. Their diversity in appearance makes them visually appealing and a wonderful conversation starter.

With so many kinds to choose from, tarantulas can be an interesting addition to any collection. Some species are better suited to beginners because of their placid disposition, but others are best suited to experienced keepers who can handle more defensive or problematic species. Whether you prefer giant, slow-moving species or smaller, faster ones, there is a tarantula to meet your tastes.

4. Educational and Therapeutic Values

Tarantulas provide valuable educational opportunities, especially for individuals interested in biology, ecology, or the natural world. Observing their behavior, morphology, and life cycle can help you better understand arachnids and invertebrates, as well as develop a respect for these often misunderstood species. Owning a tarantula can be a great opportunity to teach youngsters about the natural world, responsibility, and the value of empathy for all living things.

Tarantulas can also provide medicinal benefits. Research has shown that spending time with pets helps relieve stress and anxiety, and caring for a tarantula can bring a sense of peace and purpose. Tarantulas' quiet, patient demeanor can be calming, and the routine of feeding and maintaining their habitat can provide structure and a sense of connection to the natural world. Furthermore, monitoring their motions and behavior can be a relaxing escape from the stresses of daily life.

5. Long life and investment in a relationship.

Tarantulas, unlike many smaller pets, can survive for decades, requiring a long-term commitment. Female tarantulas, in particular, can live for up to 30 years in some situations, providing years of companionship as well as the opportunity to witness a tarantula's development and life cycle. This extended lifetime makes them a good choice for people who are willing to make a long-term commitment in their pet's care and well-being.

Tarantulas have a lengthy lifespan, which helps owners to build deeper bonds with their pets over time. Many owners describe building a special bond with their tarantulas as they learn more about their habits and requirements. Watching a tarantula grow and thrive in your care can be a tremendously rewarding experience since you get to see the life of a unique and intriguing creature develop.

Final Tips for Long-Term Care

Owning a tarantula may be a very gratifying experience, but to ensure that your pet has a long, healthy, and happy life, you must provide regular care and attention. Here are some final advice for the long-term care of your tarantula.

1. Provide an appropriate enclosure.

The most crucial component of tarantula care is creating an appropriate environment. Your tarantula's habitat should be spacious enough to allow them to roam freely, with sufficient dirt for digging, hiding locations, and access to water. Tarantulas are superb escape artists, so ensure that the enclosure is properly secured. Additionally, make sure that the enclosure is kept at the appropriate temperature and humidity for your species, since environmental conditions can have a big impact on their health.

2. Keep Feeding Simple and Consistent.

Tarantulas require little upkeep in terms of food. Most species can live on a diet of adequately sized insects like crickets, mealworms, and roaches. Make sure to provide live food that is not too big for your tarantula to manage, and remove any uneaten prey after 24 hours to avoid contamination. Feed your tarantula once or twice a week, depending on its size, age, and species.

It is also critical to give fresh water at all times. A modest water dish or a small, wet sponge can be utilized to provide your tarantula with access to water while avoiding drowning.

3. Be patient and respectful.

Tarantulas are solitary species who enjoy little interaction, therefore it's critical to respect their boundaries. Many tarantulas are naturally nervous and will not tolerate repeated handling or disruption. If you wish to engage with your tarantula, do so cautiously and only when it is appropriate. This will make your tarantula feel safe and secure in its environment, lowering stress and preventing harm.

If you intend to breed your tarantulas, make sure you understand the special breeding behaviors of the species you own. Breeding tarantulas may be a difficult and delicate procedure, so thoroughly research the needs of both the male and female before attempting to mate them.

4. Monitor health and molting.

Regularly observe your tarantula's activity, feeding habits, and molting cycles to ensure its health. Tarantulas will molt multiple times during their lifetimes, and each molt should go well. If your tarantula exhibits signs of sickness, such as lethargy, loss of appetite, or discolouration, consult a reptile or arachnid veterinarian.

During the molting process, avoid upsetting your tarantula because it is a sensitive time for the animal. Ensure that the enclosure is at the proper humidity level for a good molt, and remove any uneaten food before the molt begins.

5. Stay informed.

As with any pet, you should be aware of your tarantula's species and maintenance requirements. Investigate any special requirements your tarantula may have, and keep up with current breakthroughs in tarantula care and rearing. Joining online communities, reading care guides, and talking with other experienced tarantula owners can all provide useful information and assist you ensure that your tarantula's needs are addressed throughout its life.

Keeping a tarantula may be a really pleasant and fulfilling experience. These intriguing critters provide a one-of-a-kind and captivating pet ownership experience, with a diverse range of species to pick from, each with their own set of behaviors, colors, and characteristics. Tarantulas can thrive in captivity with adequate care, patience, and respect, providing years of fun for their owners.

Tarantula ownership comes with more benefits than just owning a pet; it also allows you to watch and admire one of the most ancient and mysterious species on Earth. A tarantula is a good choice if you want a low-maintenance pet, a captivating friend, or a long-term relationship with a unique species.

You may reap the benefits of tarantula ownership for years to come by creating the correct environment, sticking to a consistent feeding schedule, and respecting your tarantula's demands.

Printed in Dunstable, United Kingdom